THE WALK

THE WALK
A JOURNEY WITH GOD

DFD 2.2 a study of how to apply your faith

A NavPress resource published in alliance
with Tyndale House Publishers

NavPress is the publishing ministry of The Navigators, an international Christian organization and leader in personal spiritual development. NavPress is committed to helping people grow spiritually and enjoy lives of meaning and hope through personal and group resources that are biblically rooted, culturally relevant, and highly practical.

For more information, visit NavPress.com.

The Walk: A Journey with God

Copyright © 2004 by The Navigators. All rights reserved.

A NavPress resource published in alliance with Tyndale House Publishers.

NAVPRESS and the NavPress logo are registered trademarks of NavPress, The Navigators, Colorado Springs, CO. *TYNDALE* is a registered trademark of Tyndale House Publishers. Absence of ® in connection with marks of NavPress or other parties does not indicate an absence of registration of those marks.

Cover design by BURNKIT
Creative Team: Eric Johnson, Gabe Filkey, Rachelle Gardner, Kathy Mosier,
    Pat Reinheimer

All Scripture quotations, unless otherwise indicated, are taken from the Holy Bible, *New International Version,*® *NIV.*® Copyright © 1973, 1978, 1984, 2011 by Biblica, Inc.® Used by permission. All rights reserved worldwide.

For information about special discounts for bulk purchases, please contact Tyndale House Publishers at csresponse@tyndale.com, or call 1-800-323-9400.

ISBN 978-1-57683-637-8

INTRODUCTION

It won't take long until you encounter it. Or maybe you've already lived with it your whole life: the bizarre way people talk to one another in church or Bible study groups. *Christianese.*

Like any subculture, Christianity has a language all its own. Spend any amount of time in church or in a youth group and, guaranteed, you'll hear stuff like, "Let's lift her up in prayer" or "producing fruit" or my pastor's favorite, "being Berean-like." *Huh?* Exactly. If you're not a card-carrying member of this exclusive group, you'll never figure out what in the world these people are saying. They're speaking Christianese.

Walk is one of those ambiguous words. You'll hear it repeatedly tossed about among Christ-followers. "How's your Walk going?" "I want to improve my Walk." But why *Walk?* The word captures the essence of our relationship with God. It's Walking, sometimes even sprinting, after Him, alongside Him, hand in hand with Him. There are times in the Walk when it seems we ride on His shoulders as if we're four years old again. But all the time, we're moving forward, exercising our faith in God and our love of Christ.

The *Walk*, while definitely Christianese, is one term we can use to capture what it means to let God's Spirit guide and transform us to become more like Christ. How do we get started Walking? Put your shoes on and let's go.

CHAPTER 1

STARTING OUT

When we finally see Christ for who He is—Savior, Master, Brother—we want to drop everything and follow Him. It's a bit like the first stages of falling in love: The roses are so red, the violets so blue, and your new love never seems to mind the really horrific poems you try to compose. But after a few weeks, some of that infatuation starts to wane as you truly get to know the person. Maybe he doesn't call when he's running late. Maybe she chews with her mouth open. All the little things we fail to notice at first start to surface as we begin to let our guard down.

But this isn't a bad thing. In fact, it's good. It wouldn't be fair to expect a relationship to resemble a far-fetched fairy tale or the canned laughter of some brainless sitcom. The Walk is the part of your spiritual life that begins after the first couple of dates—when you can begin to be yourself with God and expose some of the ugly or less-than-perfect qualities you have. As in any relationship, there comes a time when you need to deal with the garbage in your life that you've been okay with but that no one else wants to deal with. You start to see that maybe some changes need to be made. Possibly you have to call a few more times. Or chew with your mouth closed. Or consider even more serious adjustments. That's part of staying in a relationship. It's also part of living the Walk.

So we do what it takes to stay close to God—to Walk with Him wherever He takes us because we trust Him and know that His plans for us are perfect, even when we don't always know what's coming next.

WHAT IS THE WALK?

1. The Walk is a common metaphor for a life set on following Christ. It implies that we are active, on the go, and ready to travel where God takes us. That's key because we can't Walk if we don't get up and move. First John 1:7 states that "if we walk in the light, as he is in the light, we have fellowship with one another, and the blood of Jesus, his Son, purifies us from all sin." According to this verse, the Walk does two things for us. What are they?

-

-

2. Try to find a few more passages that refer to Walking with God. If your Bible has a concordance, start there; if it doesn't, use an online concordance, like www.biblegateway.com, and do a keyword search for *walk*. What else can you learn about the Walk from some of these passages?

3. Pick one of the verses you found. Explain what it says about the Walk.

4. Walking isn't the only way to describe the life of a God-follower. The Bible uses other parallels from our physical life to illustrate our

spiritual life. For instance, just as we need daily nourishment from food, we also need regular spiritual sustenance from God's Word. Another analogy is that we are children of a Father in heaven, just as we are children of our earthly fathers. Think of a couple more real-life comparisons and write them down.

-

-

5. Walking should lead to progress as we advance in our relationship with God. What happens if we don't grow as we Walk (Ephesians 4:14)?

6. Later, in verses 22-25 of the same chapter, Paul wrote that a relationship with Christ should change who we are if our Walk is going to mean anything. Use these verses to contrast in three ways the person you were with the person you are becoming.

Old You   **New You**

-

-

-

7. So why do all of these changes need to take place? What's the point (Ephesians 2:10)?

8. The book of Romans is one of the most thorough clarifications of what our Walk with God is all about. Read between the lines, if you will, of the following verses. Each one relates to some aspect of our Walk with Christ.

   a. Romans 5:6: How is the Walk even possible in the first place?

   b. Romans 6:22-23: We used to be slaves to sin—our only option was to mess up. Now, we gladly leave all that behind and become "slaves" to God. (Note: Here, "slaves" means that our only option is to do the right things and follow God, as opposed to our previous slavery to doing the wrong things.) What is the result of our "slavery" to God?

   c. Skip ahead a couple of chapters to Romans 8:5. How does this verse relate to our Walk with God?

d. Walking is exercise, and exercise isn't always easy. How can we be sure that our hard work—our "sufferings"—will pay off in the end (Romans 8:16-18)?

9. Give an example from your own life when you experienced how the Walk pays off.

The Walk consists of three primary stages: (1) justification, (2) sanctification, and (3) glorification.

Justification occurred when we accepted Christ and He set us right with God. It happened once—past tense—and will never need to happen again. Jesus' death and resurrection were enough.

Sanctification, you might remember from *The Life*, isn't a one-time event, but a process. It happens to some degree every moment we live. The Spirit guides, leads, and prompts us in our day-to-day living to become more and more like Christ and to reflect His glory. This is truly the essence of the Walk—getting further and further away from our old ways ("slave to sin") and choosing more and more to align ourselves with God, trusting Him and staying in a close relationship with Him ("slave to God").

Glorification is what we have to look forward to—an eternity with Christ, free from all of our tendencies to wander away. It's difficult to imagine just how different and incredible this will be; we'll need new bodies and new senses to adequately experience an all-impressive, all-beautiful, and all-perfect God.

The following chart recaps the differences among these three stages of the Walk.

Justification	*Past* Tense—I have been saved . . . from the penalty of sin.	My *position* is in Christ.
Sanctification	*Present* Tense—I am being saved . . . from the power of sin.	My *condition* is becoming like Christ.
Glorification	*Future* Tense—I will be saved . . . from the presence of sin.	My *expectation* is to be like Christ.

All this goes to show that the Walk—while it definitely requires effort, practice, even suffering—pays off in the end. God is genuinely good to those who Walk with Him, who stay strong, persevere, and reflect His glory.

10. Look up Colossians 3:1-4. How do these verses relate to all three parts of the preceding chart?

11. You may have noticed by now that this Walk isn't your typical stroll through the park. You definitely need to attain varying levels of skill and discipline as you learn how to truly Walk. Read Romans 6:11-13 and try to apply these principles to your Walk.

a. What part of you has died?

b. Because of this, who or what should rule your life?

c. How can you accomplish this? What real steps can you take to Walk toward God?

12. It's always good to be reminded of the reason we Walk. Why do we do all these crazy things like "count ourselves dead" to our old ways and instead become "slaves to God"? We do it because we realize how much God loves us and what He did for us, and we want to do everything we can to be with Him and share His goodness with everyone we know (1 John 3:1-3). Write out a prayer to God explaining why you want to Walk with Him. (Note: If you're not sure you want to Walk with God, talk with Him about it. Tell Him you *want* to want to Walk with Him. Ask Him to give you that desire.)

HOW SHOULD I WALK?

13. In Micah 6:8, we are given explicit directions about how the Father wants us to Walk. Look up this verse to help you answer the following questions.

   a. List the three things God requires of us.

   -
   -
   -

   b. Why do you think the Father tells us *how* we are supposed to Walk?

   c. Of these three requirements related to the Walk, which is the most difficult for you personally? Why?

14. Look up the following verses. How does each one say we should Walk?

   Romans 8:4:

   2 Corinthians 5:7:

Ephesians 5:1-2:

1 John 2:6:

15. Stay in 1 John if you haven't already lost your page. Read 2:15-17. What are some practical ideas you can take from this passage and apply to your Walk? Do you already know of a few things that might be tripping you up as you try to Walk with God?

16. What role do our God-following friends and family play in our Walk? What role do we play in theirs (Hebrews 10:23-25)?

17. Now turn to Romans 12:1-2. What two things are Christ-followers called to do?

-

-

18. Rewrite this passage in your own words. (Be sure to relate it to your Walk with God.)

19. Fortunately, as you might remember from *The Life*, we aren't alone in this Walk. We have Someone who helps us stay strong and know what's right and what's not. Who is it, and how does He come into our lives? (If you need a reminder, look up 2 Corinthians 1:21-22.)

WHERE WILL THIS WALK TAKE ME?

20. Jesus is our prime example. He Walked perfectly, even when it ended in His brutal assassination. Because of this, Jesus gets all the credit, all the glory. Eventually, every person who has ever lived will give Christ His due, because His perfect Walk made it possible for us to be God's own children. Those who rejected Christ will realize what a huge mistake they made. For more on this, examine Philippians 2:6-11.

   a. What traits defined Christ's Walk on earth?

   b. How, exactly, will people respond when they see Christ in all His glory?

   c. Why has God given Jesus so much honor (verses 6-9)?

21. Now look back one verse to Philippians 2:5. How does this statement (and everything you read in question 17) frame the way you think about the Walk?

22. Christ's example shows us the quintessential way to Walk. He Walked with humility, even when the terrain was treacherous and people wanted to kill Him. When the going gets tough for us, the Walk can feel more like a race—as though we're running for our lives like some freaked-out blonde in a horror movie. When it feels like this, remember this passage: Hebrews 12:1-3.

    a. What four things are we supposed to do, according to this passage?

-

-

-

-

    b. What is Christ's role in all of this?

c. How can we keep from growing tired of our Walk (verse 3)?

*Extra Credit: Memorize Hebrews 12:1-3. Start by writing it out a couple of times. Then say it to your friend, your dog, whomever. It's a passage that can help you time and time again on your Walk.

23. Jesus said in Luke 9:23 that if we want to Walk with Him, we must carry our cross daily and follow Him. What does it mean to carry our cross? What does that look like in your life?

24. Read the rest of what Jesus said in Luke 9:24-26. What does it mean to you to lose your life for Jesus' sake? How is this a part of your Walk? Did Jesus lose His life for anybody's sake?

25. One more time: Why do you Walk?

   a. For something to do.
   b. Everyone tells me to.
   c. Otherwise I'll feel guilty.
   d. Because I love God so much.
   e. For some other reason: _____

26. Explain your answer.

SUMMARY

Walking with God means living out our faith actively and purposefully. It is how we progress, grow up, and become a brighter reflection of Christ's glory. But at the same time, it isn't just a walk in the park. This Walk looks more like an expedition, like something out of Tolkien's trilogy or Bunyan's *Pilgrim's Progress*. Where God will lead us in this life is anyone's guess — that's part of the excitement. Where we will ultimately end up, however, is in heaven, in glory, with Christ. That's something to remember.

CHAPTER 2

ALONG THE WAY

Sometimes it would be nice if the Walk were along a clearly designated, well-lit Yellow Brick Road. You could frolic along, meeting new Tin Man friends on your way to the Father. Nothing could be easier. You'd have no major decisions to make; you'd just stay on the path and the strange flying monkeys wouldn't get you.

But no, this Walk is more like climbing to the top of Everest without a Sherpa to help you (unless you call the Spirit your Sherpa, which really isn't sound theology). Your Journey will not look exactly like anyone else's Journey. And there's (thankfully) no standard brick road that everyone must travel. Instead, God gives us myriad opportunities to follow Him creatively and intuitively. But with this freedom come huge responsibilities. For instance, you must trust God more than you trust anyone else, even yourself.

Jesus said, "Wide is the gate and broad is the road that leads to destruction, and many enter through it. But small is the gate and narrow the road that leads to life, and only a few find it" (Matthew 7:13-14). In other words, our Walk is an expedition—a rugged, gritty pilgrimage with God—on which most people never dare to embark. But in faith, Christ-followers take the chance and Walk.

WALKING BY FAITH

1. What is faith (Hebrews 11:1)?

2. Without faith, you wouldn't take even the first step in your Walk. Without faith, you wouldn't believe in Christ, and you definitely wouldn't spend your time studying how to follow Him. Faith is central to the Walk because we don't have all the answers up front. With this in mind, explain how 2 Corinthians 5:7 affects the way you Walk. (See also 2 Corinthians 4:18.)

3. Find Habakkuk 2:4. This verse clues us in very specifically to how God wants His children to Walk—and how He doesn't want us to Walk. List the two contrasting ways below.

-

-

4. Walking by faith isn't impossible, even though "seeing the unseen" and "living by faith, not by sight" can sometimes sound confusing. To help us "see" what God means by these esoteric statements, we have practical examples of how to Walk by faith. Hebrews 11 is like the Faith Hall of Fame—these men and women Walked by faith and did things right. Read this chapter and pick your favorite faith celebrity. Then write why this person impressed you and how you can try to Walk like him or her.

FAITH IS ROOTED IN A PROMISE

5. The Bible is full of God's promises, all of which are meant to help us Walk in confidence and faith. What does the Bible say about God's promises?

   1 Kings 8:56:

   Psalm 89:34:

   Isaiah 55:11:

   2 Peter 1:4:

6. What do you think: Can you trust God's promises? Why or why not?

7. One of the best ways to utilize these powerful promises is to pray them back to God, saying, "God, You said _____, and I believe You are always true to Your Word." Though God always

keeps His promises, He sometimes attaches conditions to them. Look up some of God's promises and fill in the chart below.

	Promise	**Condition, If Any**
John 15:7:		
Lamentations 3:22-23:		
Romans 8:28:		
Galatians 6:7:		

8. Why do you think God makes some of His promises conditional on our behavior and attitude (Hebrews 6:12)?

9. Stay in Hebrews 6 and look at verses 16-20. The writer said people make promises like, "I swear by my mother's grave . . ." to show others how serious they are about what they're saying. But when God makes a promise, He says, "I swear by Me," because He is the be-all and end-all—there's no greater guarantee. How does this fact relate to the Walk?

10. Review some of God's promises that you looked up earlier. Is there one verse that you think will be especially helpful to you on your Walk?

FORKS IN THE ROAD

Tough times will come—I promise.

11. As we Walk, it's crucial to know what God has promised us, especially as we come upon unexpected forks in the road. According to Psalm 32:8, how will God guide us?

12. Analyze Philippians 4:13. What can you learn from this verse that will help you Walk with confidence, even when you aren't sure what to do?

13. Forks in the road can sometimes come in the form of decisions with moral consequences. Whether it's about deciding how to spend your time, making friends, or setting boundaries with your girlfriend or boyfriend, finding God's will usually requires you to get in the right frame of mind. Look at David's perspective in Psalm 40:8 and answer the following questions.

a. Where did David store God's Law (His promises and words)?

b. In what ways do you think this resolute attitude helped David Walk with confidence?

c. Is this frame of mind possible for you? Explain your answer.

14. You can have the best of intentions and even the right frame of mind. But when push comes to shove, what really matters is how you implement God's will into your Walk. James 1:22-25 talks about two contrasting types of people. Write down some of the differences between them.

Type 1	**Type 2**

15. Evaluate how successfully you think Type 1 and Type 2 will Walk with God, especially when they encounter unforeseen obstacles.

16. Look at the following examples from the Bible and answer these questions: What decision was made? What was the outcome, as far as you can tell? Was it the right move to make?

Person	Decision	Outcome	Right/Wrong

Gideon
(Judges 6:25-28):

Moses
(Hebrews 11:24-26):

Demas
(2 Timothy 4:10):

17. Faith keeps us going through all the trials and dramas of life. Look again at questions 11-16. Try to summarize some important things you can keep in mind when Walking through tough times, specifically some of the grueling, confusing times you've already encountered or foresee in the near future.

18. When you're really stumped about how or where God wants you to Walk, ask yourself the following useful questions to help you figure out the best of all options. Pick one decision you've recently made or

will soon be making and answer these questions. If you can answer "yes" to each of them, you're probably Walking along the right path.

- Does your decision align with what the Bible teaches?
- Do your prayers support your decision?
- Does the advice of your Christian friends and mentors support your decision?
- Have your circumstances made it possible to act out your decision?
- Having reached this decision, do you have a sense of inner peace about it?*

19. When you are confident that you have discovered God's will, how should you live it out (Ephesians 6:7-8)?

REMEMBERING WHO IT'S FOR

20. All this stuff can start to sound like a to-do list if we don't remember the reason we Walk: It's about loving Jesus. Explain what motivates your Walk with God.

---

*This advice comes from another TH1NK book called *Destination Unknown* by Gordon S. Jackson.

21. When we look at how Jesus Walked, He amazes us once again. What characteristic defined Christ's Walk? Why does this matter (Mark 10:45)?

22. Though they were with Him all the time, Jesus' disciples didn't always understand this. Read Luke 22:24-27 and answer the following questions.

    a. What were the disciples arguing about?

    b. How did Jesus make their argument seem petty?

    c. If you want to be "great," how should you Walk (verse 26)?

    d. How does this attitude compare to the way people typically think?

23. You may be wondering, *What does this attitude look like in real life?* To find out, answer these questions in your mind:

- If God asked you to do so, could you bite your tongue if everyone else was gossiping about someone who always gossips about you?
- Could you give up your social status if it was interfering with your relationship with God?
- Could you serve God by scrubbing toilets if that's what He wanted you to do?
- Could you Walk with Christ if it meant you would be ridiculed or ostracized?

24. Now, write your own question that relates to your life and answer it honestly.

These questions might sound weird, but they're all valid. When we Walk with God, we must be ready for anything. Christ was—even to the point of torture and death.

25. Being humble for any extended period of time is right up there with neurosurgery and experimental mathematics on the difficulty scale; our human nature just doesn't naturally work that way. And yet that's exactly how we are supposed to Walk. Look up Philippians 2:3-4. What would you have to do to make these characteristics a defining part of your Walk?

26. List some specific ways you can Walk more like Christ.

SUMMARY

The Walk is full of God's never-ending goodness and promises. We Walk by faith—in love and humility—because we value God above all else. We need to be humble enough to admit that we won't always have the answers up front. This Journey will lead us to become more like Christ every day—if we aren't daunted by the rigors and challenges of the path before us.

CHAPTER 3

A GOOD WALK TO CLEAR OUR HEADS OF BAD IDEAS

Maybe you get those ridiculous e-mails with the earth-shattering news that the world is going to end unless you forward a message to ten people. Perhaps they ask you to sign a petition to stop baby tiger torture before it's too late or to make a wish or take a quiz that will define your personality. There are literally thousands of urban legends and Internet hoaxes just waiting for some gullible person to forward them to everyone in his or her address book. The information age brings with it plenty of misinformation.

Christianity is no different. Some people distort or twist the truth in such a way that the real, radical truth of Christ becomes nothing but a rabbit hole to nowhere. Don't believe it. The Walk orbits around our love of Christ, treasuring Him above all else — nothing more, nothing less. He encompasses all of our hopes, dreams, and greatest ideas. Any Walk less than this is a myth. Don't fall for it. And definitely don't forward it on to your friends.

MYTH 1: WE WALK TO BE SERVED.

As you've seen, Christ's perfect Walk consisted of supernatural humility, not luxury. Yet so many people think that following God is their "golden ticket" to health, wealth, and prosperity — as if God is some genie who grants them their every wish. Sorry, that's a myth.

1. Here's a quick review. Go back to Philippians 2 and read verses 5-8. How did Jesus live His life?

2. Paul debunked this myth in a hurry in Romans 6:22.

   a. What analogy did he use to describe our relationship with God?

   b. Would you say this is a good way to think about our Walk with Christ? Why or why not?

   c. How does this compare with the myth that God is our eternal Santa Claus?

3. Even though we have given up sin and aligned ourselves with God, serving Christ and others isn't easy. We still must choose to serve Him instead of our old ways. Read how Joshua challenged his countrymen in Joshua 24:14-15. Does this verse still apply to our Walk today? Why or why not?

4. Jesus showed His disciples what the Walk is all about by washing their feet. Why did He do this (John 13:13-16)?

5. Warning: Don't blow it by serving God (and others) while secretly believing that you are the greatest person ever. Likewise, don't take pride in not having any pride—that's just as big a myth as any other. When we're doing a good job, what attitude does Christ say we should have (Luke 17:10)?

6. According to Luke 16:10, why do the "little things"—like always serving with the right attitude—matter so much?

7. Name one way you can make serving others an everyday part of your Walk.

MYTH 2: WE'RE SAVED! PARTY ON!

This is one of the oldest myths in the (Good) Book. Paul addressed this issue because some people were under the impression that they could do whatever they wanted because they were saved by God's grace. They didn't understand that trusting Christ as their Savior is just the beginning of the Walk, not the end.

Because many of the people during His time lived off the land, Jesus used an example from the horticultural world to describe how we should live. It goes like this: Suppose you are a branch on a great orange tree. God owns the tree. Orange trees are supposed to do what? Make oranges. What happens if one branch on the tree doesn't make any oranges? It meets an ugly death with a chainsaw.

8. Meditate on John 15:1-8. Explain how "bearing fruit" relates to your Walk with Christ.

9. Revisit this passage. It doesn't just command us to be "fruitful"; it also tells us how to accomplish that—and it may not be what you would think. What is the secret to being productive for God's glory? (Hint: Look at verses 4 and 5.)

10. What does this "fruit" look like (Galatians 5:22-23)?

11. The Bible talks about several aspects of our lives in which these traits should be displayed. Explain how the following verses relate to your Walk.

Philippians 4:8:

Colossians 4:6:

1 Peter 2:12:

12. According to Luke 6:45, which of these three areas is most important to a productive Walk? Explain why you agree or disagree.

13. Next, read 2 Peter 1:1-9. Read it a couple of times, if possible. This passage is full of incredible advice on how to Walk with Christ without lapsing into laziness.

    a. First of all, summarize Peter's main point.

    b. How is it possible to Walk in godliness (verses 3-4)?

    c. List the qualities mentioned in verses 5-7. How do these compare to the list in question 10?

d. Verse 8 says we are to "possess these qualities in increasing measure." Why?

14. Don't fall for the myth that saying a simple prayer is all that is necessary to follow Christ. Learn to recognize a myth when you hear one. Read James 3:13-18. Contrast the two types of wisdom.

Type 1   **Type 2**

MYTH 3: I KNOW WHAT LOVE IS.

All people can love those who love them. Loving those you don't like is another issue. But that's what being a Christ-follower is all about—loving others, even those who despise you, more than you love yourself.

15. *Love.* Such a nice, totally misunderstood word. What does the Bible say love is and isn't (1 Corinthians 13:4-8)?

Is   **Isn't**

16. Much of what we know about love comes from one writer in particular: John. He showed off his quasi-obsession with love in 1 John 4:7-21. (On a side note, whenever an author repeats one concept ad nauseam, we should expect to hear something important. This passage is no exception.)

    a. How many times did John use the word *love*?

    b. According to verses 8 and 16, "God is_____."

    c. How does this change your definition of love?

    d. Why do we love God, or anyone else for that matter (verse 19)?

17. According to each of the following passages, who should Christ's followers love?

   Deuteronomy 6:5:

   Luke 6:27:

   1 Peter 4:8:

18. The way we talk to people is one way we can show that we love them. Pick *one* of the proverbs below and explain what the right kind of words can mean to a person.

   Proverbs 12:25:

   Proverbs 16:24:

   Proverbs 22:11:

19. Love means that we think of others before ourselves (Romans 12:9-10). Why is this such an important aspect of the Walk?

20. Go back to 1 John. Read chapter 3, verses 16-18.

   a. Are you ready, with help from the Holy Spirit, to love other people in this way? Why or why not?

   b. Write out a couple of practical ways you can show God's love to people you know.

21. Love is mandatory if we are going to Walk with God. Not the phony Hollywood version of love, but sincere, caring action for people. This type of love comes only from the Father. Summarize how God (and His love) is revealed in our lives, according to 1 John 4:11-12.

SUMMARY

Know what the Walk is. Don't fall into the trap of believing it is anything less than a life-defining relationship with God. Look to serve, not to be served—despite what you hear from TV evangelists. Don't fall for the lie that Walking won't cost you anything—it cost Jesus His life. Love God and others more than you love yourself. Christ loves you; share His love. Debunking these myths will keep you Walking in the right direction.

CHAPTER 4

TAKING A STAND WHILE YOU WALK

Taking a stand while you walk is an oxymoron. It implies a static, immobile state of being and at the same time a kinetic, fluid action. Like so much about God and His ways, it's a paradox we live with.

We need to take a stand—to know what we believe and why. But if we only take a stand and never grow, we can unknowingly become dogmatic hypocrites who have never learned to do anything but repeat what we've been told.

We need to Walk to stretch ourselves and to acquire new perspectives and insights. But if we only Walk and aren't grounded in the truth, we run the risk of Walking right into the sophisticated trap of some half-baked theory.

So we learn to do both—to stretch ourselves in such a way that we always need God and to understand that we must humbly live up to everything we know and say to be true.

1. Read Jeremiah 17:9.

   a. How does this verse explain why it's sometimes so difficult to Walk with God?

b. Can you name a time when you tried to rationalize something you did that you knew was wrong? (You probably won't have to think too hard.)

c. Can you see God changing your heart? In what ways?

2. Can we change our own hearts? Can we figure it out by ourselves? Why or why not (Romans 3:10-12)?

3. As we Walk, it's easy to get comfortable—to feel as if everything is under control. We can forget that without Christ, we are totally lost. According to Romans 12:3, what should our attitude be?

4. Having the right perspective as we Walk helps us maintain a real appreciation for the Spirit's role in our lives; it also keeps us humble so we can better relate to others. With that in mind, why are all Christ-followers motivated to change (2 Corinthians 5:14-15)?

5. Because we know where we've come from, we also know how easily we can fall back into habits that make it impossible to Walk. Read 2 Corinthians 8:21 and Acts 24:16.

   a. How did Paul ensure that he didn't revert to his old ways?

   b. What can you learn from Paul's example?

6. So be smart about your new and your old identity. Don't wander back to your old ways, or you could find your Walk detoured indefinitely. By what means are we "dragged away and enticed" to sin (James 1:13-14)?

7. All of these passages underscore one thing: We need Christ if we truly want to Walk. Don't be a self-righteous hypocrite, thinking you've got it all figured out. It's a dangerous way to live, as Christ warned about in Mark 7:6-8. Read this passage and infer from it how you might avoid falling into a black hole of hypocrisy.

BREAKOUT SESSION: SEX

One of life's biggest temptations, especially for young people, is sexual sin. There are pressures all around, urging us to give into lustful desires that will seriously derail our Walk. The next few questions take on the issue of sex because it is possible to Walk with God, take a stand for purity, *and* remain a healthy, normal, sexual creature. After all, God made people to be sexual beings— in the proper context.

8. First things first: It's normal to think about and want sex. Having said that, it's not okay to be obsessed or impatient with it. Sexual sin will undoubtedly disrupt your Journey with God. Read 1 Thessalonians 4:3-7. As far as your sexual nature is concerned, how does God want you to Walk?

9. Purity is probably the least sexy word in the English language. But there's a big difference between "purity" and "prude-ity." Purity can

be very attractive; it means that someone has enough resolve, confidence, and faith to stay true to his or her beliefs. It's much different than just being a frumpy old prude.

    a. How would you define purity?

    b. On a scale of 1 to 10, 1 being never and 10 being practically every minute, how often do you encounter sexual temptation?

    1   2   3   4   5   6   7   8   9   10

    c. According to Ephesians 5:3, why should we take such a strong stand against sexual temptation?

10. Now look at the example of two people from the Bible who had very different ways of dealing with sexual temptation. Read Genesis 39:6-12 and 2 Samuel 11:1-5 and compare how Joseph and David fared in this area of life.

	Joseph	**David**
a. What was the temptation?		

	Joseph	**David**
b. How did he deal with it?		
c. What was the result?		
d. Speculate about why these two men responded so differently to a similar temptation.		

11. In case you're wondering, there's a really great place for sex: *marriage*.

    a. Why did God make marriage (Genesis 2:18,23-24)?

b. What does it represent (Ephesians 5:31-33)?

*Extra Credit: Put away the campy romance novels for a minute and read the "racy" book in the Bible, Song of Songs. Discuss it with a mentor, a friend, or even your parent. Talk about why sex, in its proper context, should be fun and enjoyable. Also talk about why sex, out of its proper context, can feel good physically but can leave behind painful scars on your soul.

12. Staying strong in this area will help you in many ways. (You won't have to worry about making babies, contracting diseases, or living with a guilty conscience.) But it's important to remember who empowers you to stay strong. Look back at your answers to questions 1-6. Why are you able to Walk away from sexual sin? (See also Philippians 4:13.)

THE CHASE: WHEN THE WALK BECOMES A SPRINT

13. When you start putting all these things together, the Walk can start to feel like a sprint—especially as you begin to chase seriously after God's perfect standard. Read 1 Corinthians 9:24-27.

    a. How are we supposed to run (verse 24)?

b. How did Paul say we should train for this marathon race (verse 25)?

c. In what ways does your Walk with Christ sometimes feel like a sprint?

14. Christ's life, death, and resurrection made it possible for us to escape the hold that our old, evil desires had over us. First Peter 1:13-16 mentions five things we should do as we run the race. List the five actions below and describe the purpose of each.

•

•

•

•

•

15. Romans 12:21 reminds us that we can overcome the temptations around us by doing good. Why is this important to remember?

16. If this race were easy, everyone would be doing it. Instead, you must battle your body into submission, as Paul wrote about in 2 Corinthians 10:3-5. How can you work to "take captive every thought"?

17. Holiness, much like purity, sounds intimidating—almost stuffy and boring. Nothing could be further from the truth. Running after holiness is the most exciting life you can live; it's the life most worth living, involving all aspects of your being—heart, soul, and mind. But it can be rough, too. Read 2 Corinthians 1:8-9.

   a. What does this passage say about the intensity of the chase?

   b. Can you personally relate to these words? Why or why not?

TIMES LIKE THESE

Being a Christ-follower doesn't exempt anybody from suffering. In fact, most of the twelve disciples were killed for what they believed, and one was put into boiling oil and survived. It's difficult for us to fathom in America, but around the world, Christians suffer every day for what they believe.

18. What does it mean to suffer for Christ?

   a. You love and praise Him, even when your brother gets cancer.
   b. You are thrown into an Iranian prison for telling someone about Jesus.
   c. Your car breaks down on the highway, and though you are frustrated, you find a way to thank God for keeping you safe.
   d. All of the above.

No need to keep you in suspense. The answer is *d. All of the above.* Many people live under the false impression that only persecution (abuse for telling others about Jesus) is suffering. Yes, persecution is suffering—perhaps the most intense kind—but all the bad things that happen in your life are also opportunities to Walk with God.

19. Romans 8:21-22 says that because of sin, our world is falling apart—things break, bodies get sick, bad things happen—yet God is still in control. Go back a couple of verses to Romans 8:17-18. What hope is there if we Walk with Christ through these times of suffering?

20. But how can God let horrible things happen? Is the Father still in control? These are important questions because many people lose

faith and stop Walking when they encounter difficult times. Try to give an answer to someone (maybe even yourself) who wants to know why bad things happen. Refer to Isaiah 45:5-7 and 46:9-10 for help.

21. What can we learn from each of the following passages about what our attitude toward suffering should be?

Romans 5:3-5:

1 Peter 4:12-13:

Acts 5:41:

Philippians 3:10-11:

22. What is the underlying attitude toward suffering in all of these verses?

23. There's no pat answer for suffering. It stinks and always will. But if we understand how crucial it is to our Walk, we can learn to be thankful that God is bigger than our circumstances; He brings good things out of the worst things. *Yes, even the worst possible suffering.* How does the promise of Romans 8:28 affect the way we Walk through these relentlessly difficult times?

24. Summarize the role of suffering in your Walk with Christ. As you do, answer this question: Why do Christ-followers have hope in suffering?

SUMMARY

The Walk is the day-to-day, minute-by-minute living out of our faith. To Walk rightly, we need to know when to take a stand and not be swayed and when to allow God to lead us—move us—to new, life-stretching experiences. The world is broken because of sin. And because of that, we will go through hard times. But looking to Christ and valuing Him above all else sets us free from losing our minds or our resolve. Christ loves us and will take care of us. We just need to keep Walking and trusting Him in every situation.

www.ingramcontent.com/pod-product-compliance
Lightning Source LLC
Chambersburg PA
CBHW052212090526
44584CB00019BA/3132